REGIONAL WILD AMERICA

UNIQUE ANIMALS OF THE PACIFIC COAST

By Tanya Lee Stone

BLACKBIRCH PRESS
An imprint of Thomson Gale, a part of The Thomson Corporation

THOMSON
GALE

Detroit • New York • San Francisco • San Diego • New Haven, Conn. • Waterville, Maine • London • Munich

THOMSON
GALE

For my unique family on the Pacific Coast!

© 2005 Thomson Gale, a part of The Thomson Corporation.

Thomson and Star Logo are trademarks and Gale and Blackbirch Press are registered trademarks used herin under license.

For more information, contact
Blackbirch Press
27500 Drake Rd.
Farmington Hills, MI 48331-3535
Or you can visit our Internet site at http://www.gale.com

ALL RIGHTS RESERVED.
No part of this work covered by the copyright hereon may be reproduced or used in any form or by any means—graphic, electronic, or mechanical, including photocopying, recording, taping, Web distribution, or information storage retrieval systems—without the written permission of the publisher.

Every effort has been made to trace the owners of copyrighted material.

Photo Credits: page 3, 7 (both), 11, 12, 14, 16, 19 Corel; page 5 © Dave G. Houser/CORBIS (bottom), © Kennan Ward/CORBIS (top); page 6 © Arthur Morris/CORBIS (left), © Galen Rowell/CORBIS (right), page 8 © Kevin Schafer/CORBIS; page 9 Tom McHugh/Photo Researchers, Inc.; page 10 © D. Robert and Lorri Franz/CORBIS; page 13 © David A. Northcott/CORBIS; page 15 Larry Minden/Minden Pictures; page 17 © Galen Rowell/CORBIS; page 18 Photodisc; page 20 Thomas and Pat Leeson/Photo Researchers, Inc. (top), © Paul A. Souders/CORBIS (bottom); page 21 © Tom Bean/CORBIS; page 22 © George D. Lepp/CORBIS

LIBRARY OF CONGRESS CATALOGING-IN-PUBLICATION DATA

Stone, Tanya Lee.
  Unique animals of the Pacific Coast / by Tanya Lee Stone.
    p. cm. — (Regional wild America)
  Includes bibliographical references and index.
  ISBN 1-56711-967-0 (hard cover : alk. paper)
  1. Animals-Pacific Coast States—Juvenile literature. I. Title II. Series: Stone, Tanya Lee. Regional wild America.

Printed in the United States of America
10 9 8 7 6 5 4 3 2 1

Contents

Introduction 4
Playful Pinnipeds 4
Bizarre Bird Bills 6
Bring Back the Birds! 8
Wild Wolverines 10
Snake Squeeze! 12
Tortoise Time 14
Elegant Elk 16
Mighty Mountain Lions 18
Bustling Beavers! 20
Watching for Whales 22
Glossary 24
For More Information 24
Index 24

Introduction

In the Pacific Coastal region, birds fly, marine life swims, and animals travel across the land. Many different animals make their homes on the Pacific Coast. Some animals are especially well known in this region.

Playful Pinnipeds

California sea lions can be seen all along the Pacific Coast. They are marine mammals. This means they are mammals that live most of their lives in the ocean. Sea lions are related to seals and walruses. All of these animals are pinnipeds, which means "fin-footed." They have both front and back flippers.

California sea lions are large animals. They are 5 to 7 feet (1.5 to 2 m) long. Adult males weigh 850 to 1,000 pounds (386 to 454 kg). Females are smaller and weigh about 200 pounds (91 kg). Most heavy marine animals that go ashore have trouble moving on land. But California sea lions are graceful both in and out of the water. Their flippers and their torpedo-shaped bodies make them expert swimmers. And they can push themselves up on their flippers and use them to walk on land!

The Pacific Coast

Sea lions eat mainly fish and squid. They dive for several minutes at a time to find food. They cannot breathe underwater and have to come to the surface for air. California sea lions are smart and social. They fish, rest, and play together. They often gather in large groups. On land, a group is called a colony. At sea, it is called a raft. Sea lions communicate with each other by making barking sounds. A group of sea lions is very noisy!

California sea lions use their flippers both to swim and to walk on land.

Bizarre Bird Bills

The tufted puffin is a bird that looks like no other! It has a large red and yellow bill. Its head is also colorful. It has yellow tufts that start behind each eye and sweep along the sides of its head. Tufted puffins also have bright orange feet. They live on the water and only come ashore to breed. The tops of tall seaside cliffs in the North Pacific are good nesting spots for puffins. There, they dig burrows in the ground with their bills and the sharp claws on their feet. A female lays one egg in her burrow.

After a puffin chick hatches, it takes forty-five to fifty days before it is ready to leave the burrow. During that time, the parents go back and forth between the sea and the burrow, bringing fish to the young. Puffins dive underwater to fish. They have strong, short wings that are good for swimming. They are not very good, though, for flying! It often takes puffins a few tries to take off. They can also be seen crash landing!

Although the wings of a tufted puffin are good for swimming, they are not very good for flying.

Like the tufted puffin, the brown pelican has a unique bill. This bird lives along the coasts of North America. It is a common sight in the Pacific Coast region. Brown pelicans are large birds and weigh 8 to 10 pounds (3.6 to 4.5 kg). Their wings stretch 6 to 7 feet (about 2 m) wide. The most noticeable thing about the brown pelican is its bill. Its bill is long and straight. It has a large pouch attached to it. The pelican dives underwater and scoops up fish with its bill. It can keep three times as much fish in its pouch as it can eat at one time!

Brown pelicans nest on islands off the coast of California. When they leave their nesting sites, they often fish off the coasts of Oregon and Washington. These birds are endangered. This means they are in danger of becoming extinct. The birds and their nesting sites are protected.

When brown pelicans dive underwater to catch fish, they eat some of them and store the rest in the large pouch attached to their bill.

Bring Back the Birds!

Two other birds in the Pacific Coastal region are also in need of protection. They are the northern spotted owl and the California condor. Northern spotted owls live in the forests of Washington, Oregon, and California. They live high in the treetops. These owls are mainly in danger from loss of habitat.

Northern spotted owls are raptors, or birds of prey. This means they hunt other animals for food. They eat flying squirrels, mice, rats, and other small rodents. They also eat insects, reptiles, and birds. Like other owls, they are excellent hunters. Unlike most owls, though, they do not have yellow eyes. The northern spotted owl's eyes are dark.

The northern spotted owl needs protection because its natural habitat is disappearing.

The California condor is the biggest land bird in North America.

The California condor is also a meat eater. But it eats animals that are already dead. This food is called carrion. The condor is the biggest land bird in North America. Its wingspan stretches more than 9 feet (nearly 3 m). It weighs between 16 and 23 pounds (7 to 10 kg) and stands up to 55 inches (140 cm) tall. This bird is easy to identify by its large black body and the orange or pink skin on its head.

In 1985, the California condor was nearly extinct. There were only nine birds known to be living in the wild. People took steps to save the condor. Today, there are more than two hundred of these birds.

With its sharp claws and teeth and excellent sense of smell and hearing, a forty-pound wolverine can kill an animal as large as a moose.

Wild Wolverines

What looks like a bear, walks like a weasel, and smells like a skunk? A wolverine! Wolverines belong to the same family as weasels and skunks. A wolverine has thick, shaggy brown fur. Two yellowish stripes run the length of its body. It marks its territory with a musky scent. Wolverines live in the mountains, high forests, and plains of California, Oregon, and Washington. In the United States, they also live in Alaska and parts of Montana and Colorado.

Wolverines are most active at night. Like other members of this family, a wolverine has short legs. Its body is low to the ground. These animals can run up to 9 miles (15 km) per hour. They are also great swimmers and climb trees quickly and easily.

Wolverines have a sharp sense of smell and excellent hearing. They are very strong. They also have powerful legs and sharp claws and teeth. All of these things make wolverines fierce hunters. Although they only weigh about 40 pounds (18 kg), a wolverine can kill a caribou or a moose! Wolverines will hunt almost anything. They eat deer, squirrels, beavers, and birds. They also eat eggs, berries, and carrion. Wolverines will protect their food from bigger animals, too. They can scare off animals as large as bears or mountain lions!

Snake Squeeze!

The pacific gopher snake lives on the West Coast from Washington to central California. These big snakes stretch between 4 to 8 feet (1.2 to 2.4 m) long! A gopher snake will take over a mammal's burrow for sleeping and nesting.

The pacific gopher snake is a carnivore. This means it mainly eats meat. Like boa constrictors, gopher snakes kill by squeezing an animal to death. They eat bats, mice, squirrels, and gophers. They also hunt lizards, small birds, and rattlesnakes.

A gopher snake protects itself by acting like the poisonous rattlesnake. This is called mimicry. The gopher snake hisses, flattens its head, and shakes its tail. Then it strikes! It is not a poisonous snake, but this mimicry works to chase enemies away.

A pacific gopher snake scares its enemies away by hissing, flattening its head, and shaking its tail, pretending to be a poisonous rattlesnake.

The desert tortoise is the state reptile of California.

Tortoise Time

Another reptile that lives in the Pacific Coastal region is the desert tortoise. It is California's state reptile. (It also lives in some parts of Arizona, Utah, and Nevada.) The desert tortoise is between 9 and 15 inches (23 to 38 cm) long. Males are usually larger than females.

Tortoises live only on land. Unlike many turtles, they do not spend time in water. Tortoises only use water for drinking or bathing. Desert tortoises do almost everything slowly. They grow, walk, and eat slowly. Desert tortoises are herbivores. This means they mainly eat plants. They like grasses and wildflowers.

Desert tortoises are able to live in the hot desert because they burrow into the ground to cool off. They have long nails for digging. They spend much of their days in these burrows. In the colder months, they rarely come out at all. The desert tortoise can live a really long life—up to one hundred years!

The desert tortoise survives in the desert heat by spending the day in a burrow it digs in the ground.

Elegant Elk

Roosevelt elk are named for Theodore Roosevelt, the twenty-sixth president of the United States. He loved nature and worked to protect it. Roosevelt elk live in the forests of the Pacific Coast. The largest group of them lives on the Olympic Peninsula in Washington. For this reason, they are sometimes called Olympic elk. These animals also live in parts of Canada.

Roosevelt elk are about eight feet tall and can weigh more than a thousand pounds.

Elk are members of the deer family. Roosevelt elk are large. They average 8 feet (2.4 m) in length and weigh 600 to 1,100 pounds (272 to 499 kg). Like other members of this family, they are herbivores. Roosevelt elk like huckleberry and blackberry plants. They also eat shrubs, grasses, and weeds. They feed in the early morning and in the evening.

Roosevelt elk are social animals and live in groups called herds. Males are called bucks. Bucks have large antlers with many tines, or branches. Each year, a male grows a new set of antlers. The antlers begin growing in the spring. By the beginning of the fall, they are fully grown. The male sheds its antlers each winter.

In the early morning and in the evening, herds of Roosevelt elk feed on shrubs, grasses, and weeds.

Like deer, elk have excellent senses of smell, sight, and hearing. Roosevelt elk move quickly and quietly through the forest. They are strong swimmers and can run up to 35 miles (56 km) per hour. All of these things help them avoid predators (animals who hunt other animals for food). The Roosevelt elk's main predator is the mountain lion.

Mighty Mountain Lions

Mountain lions are common in the mountains and forests of the Pacific Coast region. They are also found in western Canada and east to Wyoming and west Texas. Other names for this animal include panther, cougar, and puma.

This large cat has tan or yellowish fur. They do not have spots. Mountain lions are 6 to 8 feet (1.8 to 2.4 m) long. Males weigh between 130 and 150 pounds (59 to 68 kg). Females are a bit lighter. They weigh 65 to 90 pounds (30 to 41 kg). Mountain lions have very long tails that stretch 22 to 38 inches (56 to 97 cm). A mountain lion's tail is tipped with black fur.

Mountain lions use their excellent senses of smell and hearing to hunt for food such as deer, beavers, or raccoons.

Mountain lions have tan or yellowish fur. Their black-tipped tails can be more than three feet long.

These cats generally stay by themselves until breeding season. During that time, a mating pair may spend two weeks together. After the cubs are born, the female raises them. She stays with her cubs for about a year and a half. The female teaches the cubs how to hunt.

Mountain lions are carnivores. They hunt alone, during the day or at night. Mountain lions prefer to eat members of the deer family. They also hunt beavers, raccoons, mice, and porcupines. Mountain lions sometimes eat birds and grasshoppers, too. They are good hunters with excellent senses of smell and hearing. Like other large cats, mountain lions will sneak up on their prey and then pounce. They can leap more than 20 feet (6 m)!

Bustling Beavers!

Beavers live in rivers and streams all over America. But only Oregon is nicknamed the Beaver State. The beaver is Oregon's state mammal. Beavers are about 24 inches (61 cm) tall and weigh between 35 and 60 pounds (16 to 27 kg). They like to eat grasses, leaves, and stems. They also eat tree sap and bark. They spend most of their lives in the water. Beavers are good swimmers and have wide, flat tails for steering. Their webbed feet help them steer, too.

A beaver is a rodent. All rodents have two pairs of incisor teeth. These sharp, chisel-like teeth are used for gnawing and chewing. The teeth grow throughout the animal's life. Rodents have to constantly chew and gnaw things to keep their teeth from getting too big!

Beavers have to gnaw and chew things constantly so their long, sharp teeth do not get too big.

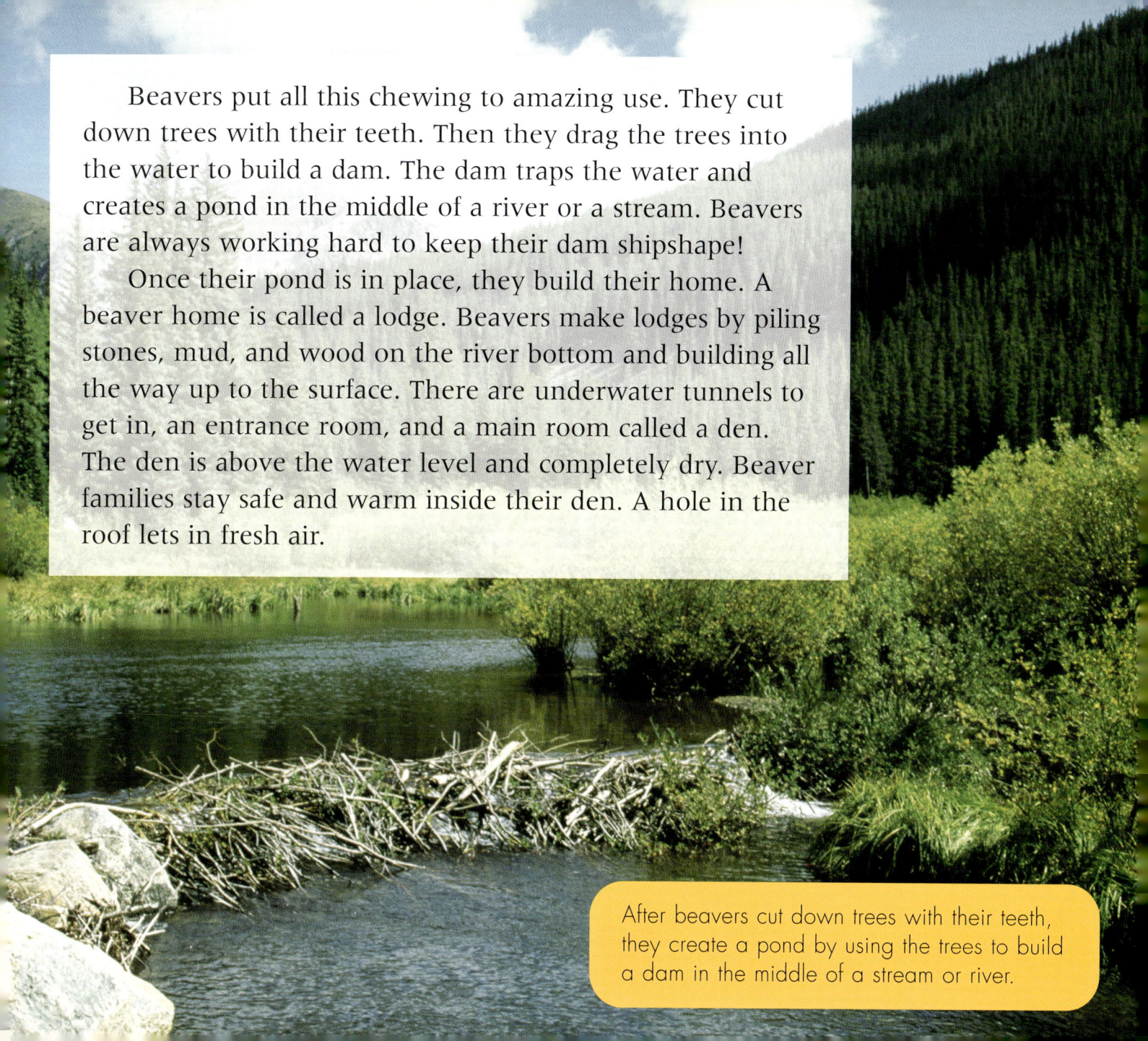

Beavers put all this chewing to amazing use. They cut down trees with their teeth. Then they drag the trees into the water to build a dam. The dam traps the water and creates a pond in the middle of a river or a stream. Beavers are always working hard to keep their dam shipshape!

Once their pond is in place, they build their home. A beaver home is called a lodge. Beavers make lodges by piling stones, mud, and wood on the river bottom and building all the way up to the surface. There are underwater tunnels to get in, an entrance room, and a main room called a den. The den is above the water level and completely dry. Beaver families stay safe and warm inside their den. A hole in the roof lets in fresh air.

After beavers cut down trees with their teeth, they create a pond by using the trees to build a dam in the middle of a stream or river.

Watching for Whales

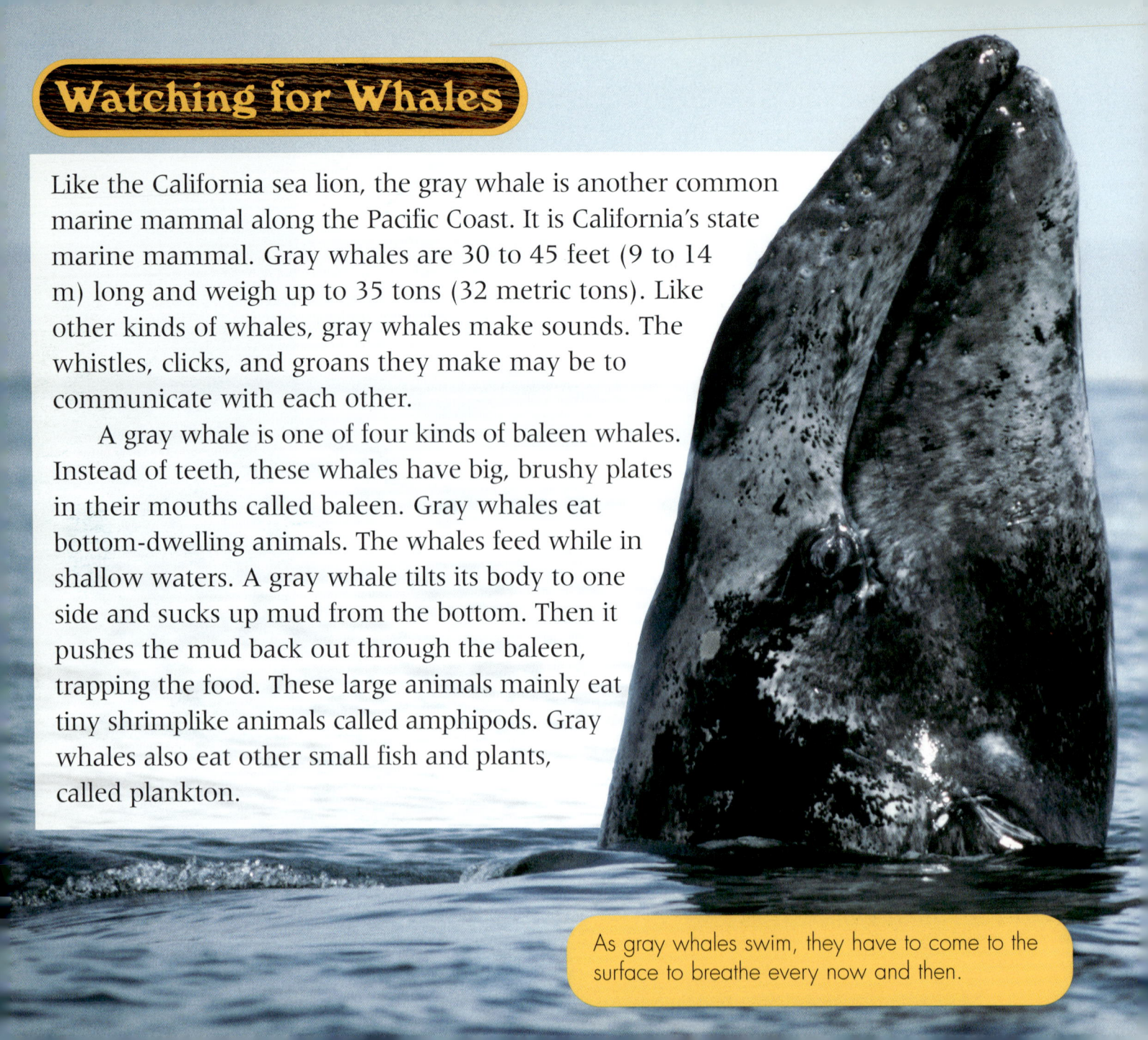

Like the California sea lion, the gray whale is another common marine mammal along the Pacific Coast. It is California's state marine mammal. Gray whales are 30 to 45 feet (9 to 14 m) long and weigh up to 35 tons (32 metric tons). Like other kinds of whales, gray whales make sounds. The whistles, clicks, and groans they make may be to communicate with each other.

A gray whale is one of four kinds of baleen whales. Instead of teeth, these whales have big, brushy plates in their mouths called baleen. Gray whales eat bottom-dwelling animals. The whales feed while in shallow waters. A gray whale tilts its body to one side and sucks up mud from the bottom. Then it pushes the mud back out through the baleen, trapping the food. These large animals mainly eat tiny shrimplike animals called amphipods. Gray whales also eat other small fish and plants, called plankton.

As gray whales swim, they have to come to the surface to breathe every now and then.

Beginning in October, gray whales leave their feeding grounds in the cold Arctic waters to travel south for the winter. As they migrate, the whales stay within a few miles of the Pacific Coast. Gray whales usually travel in small groups of two or three. People often watch for gray whales, waiting to catch a glimpse of them diving or swimming. (Unlike a humpback or blue whale, a gray whale does not have a top, or dorsal, fin. One way to spot a gray whale is by the lack of its top fin.) When the whales reach the warm waters off the coast of Mexico, they mate and have their babies.

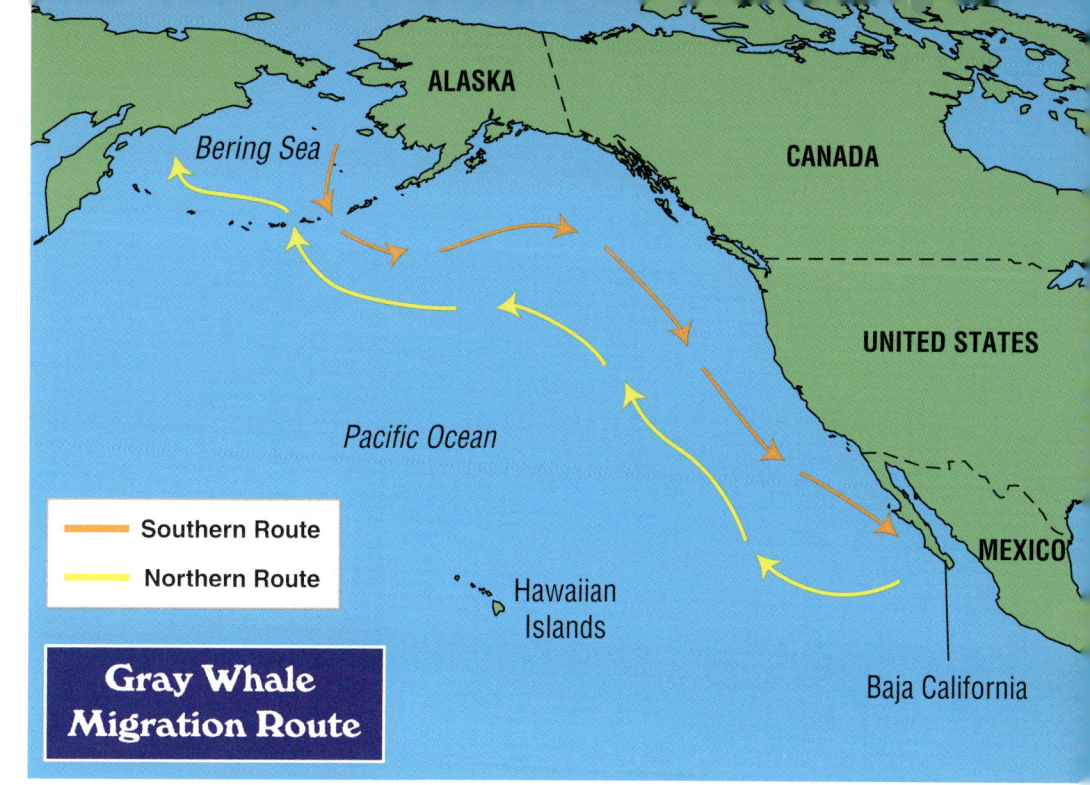

Like other marine mammals, gray whales must come to the surface to breathe. They do this through a pair of blowholes on the top of their head. Gray whales sometimes jump right out of the water! This is called breaching. They also poke their heads a few feet out of the water to take a look around. This is called spy hopping.

There are many unique and wonderful animals that live in the Pacific Coast region. All of them add to the richness and beauty of this area.

Glossary

Baleen Large brushlike structures in a baleen whale's mouth.
Carnivore An animal that mainly eats meat.
Herbivore An animal that mainly eats plants.
Predator An animal that hunts another animal for food.
Raptor A bird that hunts and kills animals for food.

For More Information

Jacobs, Lee. *Deer.* San Diego, CA: Blackbirch Press, 2002.

Scrace, Carolyn and Salariya, David. *The Journey of a Whale.* Danbury, CT: Franklin Watts, 2000.

Stone, Tanya Lee. *Sea Lions.* San Diego, CA: Blackbirch Press, 2003.

Welsbacher, Anne. *Flying Brown Pelicans.* Minneapolis, MN: Lerner, 1999.

Index

Antlers, 17

Beavers, 20–21
Bills, 6–7
Birds, 6–7, 8–9
Breaching, 23
Breeding, 6, 19
Brown pelican, 7
Burrow, 6, 12, 15

California condor, 9
California sea lions, 4–5
Condor, 9

Dam, 21

Desert tortoise, 14–15

Elk, 16–17
Extinction, 7, 9

Feet, 6, 20
Fin, 23
Flippers, 4
Fur, 11, 18

Gopher snake, 12–13
Gray whale, 22–23

Hunting, 11, 19

Marine mammals, 4–5, 22–23
Mimicry, 12
Mountain lion, 17, 18–19

Northern spotted owl, 8

Owls, 8

Pacific gopher snake, 12–13
Pelican, 7
Pinnipeds, 4–5
Pouch, 7

Puffin, 6

Roosevelt elk, 16–17

Sea lions, 4–5
Senses, 11, 17, 19
Snakes, 12–13
Spotted owl, 8

Teeth, 11, 20–21
Tortoise, 14–15
Tufted puffin, 6

Whales, 22–23
Wings, 6, 7, 9
Wolverines, 10–11